M000074076

THE
GLORY
OF THE
CROSS

EXPLORING THE MEANING OF
THE DEATH OF CHRIST

Lausanne Library

THE GLORY OF THE CROSS

**EXPLORING THE MEANING OF
THE DEATH OF CHRIST**

JAMES PHILIP

FOREWORD BY SINCLAIR B FERGUSON

The Glory of the Cross: Exploring the Meaning of the Death of Christ

Hendrickson Publishers Marketing, LLC
P. O. Box 3473
Peabody, Massachusetts 01961-3473

ISBN 978-1-61970-758-0

Printed in the United States of America

First Printing—March 2016

This booklet, edited and expanded by kind permission, is based on sermons preached in Holyrood Abbey Church, Edinburgh, Scotland under the title 'The meaning of the death of Christ'.

First published in the UK as a Didasko File 2008. Reprinted 2008, 2009, 2010, 2012. Revised and expanded 2013. All rights reserved.

Royalties have kindly been donated to support the publishing ministry of the Lausanne Movement.

Cover design by John Ruffin

FOREWORD

From time to time a publication appears, of
modest size and author, its value greater than
a whole bookshelf of contemporary bestsellers.
The Glory of the Cross falls in this category.

Its theme is so profound that a lifetime de-
voted to its study could not exhaust it. It is, essen-
tially, a simple theme, the story of the passion of
Jesus of Nazareth. But it is more than a story; it is
an explanation of what happened, and why—and,
indeed, why it *needed* to happen.

The fine quality of James Philip's mind will
immediately be obvious. But his writing is also
full of pathos. He is at one with his subject, and
has clearly been more deeply impacted by it than
by anything else in the world.

Yet there is nothing sensational here, nothing
esoteric. No hidden code is disclosed. But there
is a spirit about these pages that makes the reader
feel that they contain the deepest secret of all history. But how? And why? And what difference
does it make? To discover that, you must read on.

I first heard James Philip when I was seven-
teen years and nine months old. The precision
of the date in my memory is a measure of the
impact he made upon me. My only regret in

sounding a small fanfare for this wonderful little book is that you cannot share that experience in person. But these pages are the next best thing.

As you read them, slowly and thoughtfully, I hope you will begin to feel something of the same debt to their author that I have felt for more than four decades. And, as James Philip himself would wish, I hope that you will feel a far greater debt, of love and faith, to the Person about whom this is written. Read on, then, and discover the glory of the cross.

Revd Prof Sinclair B Ferguson
Professor of Systematic Theology,
Redeemer Seminary, Dallas, TX
Associate Preacher, St Peter's Church
Dundee, Scotland

START HERE

The final 24 hours of the Lord Jesus's life on earth are a 'holy of holies' in scripture. The gospel writers give us detailed accounts of people who were with him at each stage, and of what was said. We also know from John's gospel how Christ prayed for us in the Garden of Gethsemane. What love! As we walk through these hours, we do so with a deep sense of awe and reverence.

This booklet is for everyone: for those who came to faith in Christ many years ago, and for those who found faith in him just recently. We will never exhaust the riches of his precious death, no matter how long we have been Christians. Lend it to friends; talk about it; but more importantly, let it lead you back into the scriptures—to reflect on the cross, and to rejoice in all that Christ's death achieved. Then it will have served its purpose.

We go first to the upper room where Jesus has gathered his disciples for their last meal together.

THE LAST SUPPER

Christ's disciples had been with him for three years, yet they still did not understand his mission—that he had been born to die. As they ate together on that Thursday evening, the eternal Son of God was able to show them why he had come, in terms they would eventually recognize.

The disciples knew their history, and celebrated the Passover every year; they had done so with Jesus at least twice already, but the connection with his death had not dawned on them. Now, as Jesus knows his betrayal is only a few hours away, he holds up the Passover bread, and then the wine, and declares 'This is my body' and 'This is my blood'. He is saying, 'Look, *this* is what I mean. I have come to deliver you from slavery. Don't you understand?' It is no coincidence that Jesus's final meal with his disciples took place during the Jewish feast of the Passover.

As we celebrate the Lord's supper in our churches today, we look back to that Thursday evening in Jerusalem, and we look further back, as Jesus and his disciples did, to the events of the Passover. It is true that there is mystery here, but mystery is not the same as mystification. It is a mystery which is meant to be understood. It was

THE PASSOVER STORY

In Exodus 12 we have the story of the Passover, which was to be celebrated with thankfulness and solemnity each year 'for the generations to come' (Exodus 12:14,42). The Israelites had lived in Egypt for 430 years, since Joseph had been appointed its governor (see Genesis chapters 41–47). Now they numbered around 600,000 men, besides women and children, and Pharaoh, king of Egypt, would not let them return home. Moses and Aaron had pleaded with him to let them go, but he refused. God sent plagues, but Pharaoh's heart remained hard. Now came the most painful plague of all: the death of every firstborn son and animal in every Egyptian household. The Lord would, however, 'pass over' the homes of the Israelite families.

In preparation for this plague, the Lord instructed Moses in detail. That month would become the first month of the Israelite year. On the tenth day each Israelite household was to select a one-year-old lamb (or kid) without defect; on the fourteenth day the animal would be slaughtered at twilight, roasted that evening, and eaten with bitter herbs and with bread made without yeast. All Israelites were to mark their homes by smearing the blood of these animals on the lintel and the doorposts.

This is how the Israelite homes would be recognized and passed over, while the Egyptian firstborn sons and animals died.

In fear, Pharaoh now drove the Israelites out of Egypt. Their dramatic journey into Sinai is recorded in Exodus 12–14. They left Egypt not just as the Israelites, but as God's covenant people.

To understand the 'new Covenant' we must understand the first Covenant. For as we remember our Lord's death in the holy communion service, we find ourselves in a long trajectory of grace, reaching forward from ancient times—from the Israelites' exodus, and their delivery from slavery.

God who arranged for the betrayal of Jesus to be on Passover night.[1]

The Israelites, brought out of bondage, were the people of God. That is the context in which God gives them the Ten Commandments, opening with the words, 'I am the Lord your God who brought you out of Egypt, out of the land of slavery. You shall have no other gods before me'. He was not just giving them laws to be obeyed, but establishing his covenant with them, the covenant described in the New Testament as 'the old covenant'.

As Christ holds up the bread and the wine, he is announcing a 'new covenant'. This new covenant is what lies behind the Apostle Paul's statement that 'if anyone is in Christ he is a new creation; the old has gone; the new has come' (2 Corinthians 5:17). Paul writes to the Christians in Ephesus, 'You who were once far away have been brought near through the blood of Christ' (Ephesians 2:13). To be 'brought near' is a technical phrase meaning to be brought into the covenant. This new covenant would also draw in those who were not Jews, but Gentiles, and in due time the gospel would spread to every continent.[2] The fulfilment of that new covenant in our lives is described by Paul in one of the richest phrases in the New Testament, 'union with Christ'.[3] We have died with him and he lives in us by his Holy Spirit. By his death we are welcomed into fellowship and into friendship with the Son of God.[4]

The betrayal

Matthew, Mark and Luke all record the story of Judas's visit to the high priest to arrange to betray him. As Mary of Bethany anoints Christ's feet with expensive perfume that Thursday afternoon, Judas objects loudly that the money could have been given to the poor. But John notes that this was not because of his concern for the poor, but because he helped himself from the money bag which was entrusted to him. After witnessing this act of devotion from Mary, he went straight out to arrange the betrayal.

As we move to the upper room, the gospel writers give us a stark and dramatic contrast of two covenants; one between Christ and his disciples, and the other between Judas and the high priest. The Lord's supper is set in the context of unspeakable intrigue and betrayal. Or to put it the other way round, unspeakable betrayal is irradiated by the beauty of the new covenant.

On one level the story of the betrayal stands as a solemn warning, and as a reminder of the consequences of sin and of how far sin can go. Judas's life had been bright with promise. He was a disciple, an Apostle, in a position of responsibility. I wonder which disciple Judas walked with as they were sent out two by two, and what the two of them spoke about along the way?

None of his fellow disciples saw what was coming. We have no suggestion in the gospels that they nudged each other and nodded towards Judas when Christ predicted that one of them would betray him. On the contrary, they all asked, 'Is it I?'

Judas had had his feet washed in the upper room by the eternal Son of God. Imagine Christ's eyes looking up at him, as he looked down in shame. John tells us that Jesus handed Judas a piece of bread, dipped in wine, before he left. This was a sign of honour, of love. How Christ yearned for this man. A love of money had overtaken him, and for all Jesus's teaching on money and possessions, his heart had remained hard, and now his avarice had gone to an unimaginable extreme. John tells us that as soon as Judas took the bread, Satan entered him (John 13:27). And then we read the fateful words: 'he went out. And it was night.'

THE GARDEN OF GETHSEMANE

Matthew, Mark and Luke all give a detailed account of Christ's agony in the Garden, but John does not even mention it.[6] Why not? Perhaps he did not feel it necessary. To John, the whole of our Lord's life on earth was suffering. Right from the beginning, his death on the cross was on his mind. For John it was humiliation and indeed agony that the Son of God should have condescended to become a man. Gethsemane was just one expression of that agony. Throughout his gospel John stresses the glory of the Son of God. To John all Christ's life on earth—including his suffering—is infused with his glory.[7] John's profound and wonderful perspective provides a key as we consider the cross.

John and Luke both emphasise that Jesus went into the Garden often. He was moving willingly towards his death and was not trying to hide; Judas would know exactly where to find him.[8] When he was ready to leave the Garden, he said 'Rise, let us go' not to escape his foes, but rather to *meet* them. He was on his way to die. His death was not something he suffered so much as something he accomplished. He chose

REFLECTING ON CHRIST'S SUFFERING

If we reflect on Christ's suffering only in a devotional manner, we miss the point. We must probe the deep questions: 'Why did he suffer? What is the meaning of the agony?' As soon as we begin to explore the *why* question, we find new vistas. We see our own conversion to Christ in a new perspective—for we see it in the context of his plan for the whole world. As we do this, we find our love for him being given a firmer basis, a doctrinal foundation— building such a foundation for our faith is the best and truest way of keeping our love for him alive.[5]

when he would be betrayed, tried, and crucified. 'What you are about to do, do quickly', he said to Judas, as if to say 'This is the time which I have appointed for you to do your dire deed.'

Christ's terrible temptation

As we know from Genesis 3, Adam sinned when he was tempted in the Garden of Eden. Christ is the 'second Adam', and he triumphed in the Garden of Gethsemane. He did not draw back from the suffering which awaited him, but like a King serving on the front line, he advanced to face the enemy.[9]

Adam was tempted in Eden; and Jesus was tempted in Gethsemane. It is important for us to grasp that Christ fought with temptation; it was a real issue for him. We are told by the writer to the Hebrews that he 'has been tempted in every way, just as we are—yet without sin.'[10] So there must have been the possibility for him of drawing back, and not dying for the sins of the world.

He had fought in the wilderness with temptation to Messiah-ship without a cross when Luke tells us 'the devil left him until an opportune time.' The devil was to return in all his terrible force in Gethsemane.[11] Sometimes the most intense temptation can come before the crisis that brings blessing, as we may know from our own experience; we see that happening here.[12]

What was the cause of Christ's dreadful agony in the Garden? He did not fear physical death; not even the horrible death of crucifixion. Many believers have faced such death, calmly and fearlessly. The spiritual burden he carried—bearing the sin of the world—is what appalled his spirit. Christ's death would not symbolize, but actually *materialize* human guilt. This explains the intensity of his feelings and the words the gospel writers use to explain them—'sorrowful and troubled', 'deeply distressed and troubled', 'overwhelmed with sorrow to the point of death'.[13]

The expression rendered 'deeply distressed and troubled' probably comes from a Greek root meaning 'away from home'. Certainly, for our Lord Jesus, it was the beginning of the horror of great darkness that would end in his cry of sheer dereliction, 'My God, my God, why have you forsaken me?'

'May this cup be taken from me'

While in Gethsemane we see Christ shrinking from his suffering, but the Apostle John records him as saying, 'Shall I not drink the cup the Father has given me?'[14] He delighted to do the Father's will, yet he naturally shrank from the awful agony of separation from God.

In the Garden he knew he had to accept his death, if atonement were to be made, yet as he is dying on the cross the following afternoon he cries out 'Why have you forsaken Me?' Christ's awareness of what was happening had become clouded. In the dereliction of being cut off from God, our Saviour had been cut off from light; here was the heart of his agony. To go through it knowing everything would turn out well would not have reached into the depths of our sinful

NO CONTRADICTION

There is no contradiction between Christ's desire to do his Father's will, while also shrinking from it.

In the book of Leviticus we read of the burnt offering (a 'sweet- savour offering' of an unblemished animal) presenting a beautiful aroma to the LORD. But there is also a 'sin offering', a different kind of sacrifice, where the animal's blood is shed to substitute for the taking of human life in punishment for sin. Here is the essence of atonement. All this foreshadows what now becomes real, and ultimate, in the offering *and* sacrifice of Christ himself. He offers to the Father a perfect life without blemish, in sheer devotion to the Father's will. And he becomes, in our place, the sacrifice for sin. This is the double truth captured in Thomas Binney's lovely hymn:

> *There is a way for man to rise*
> *To that sublime abode:*
> *An offering and a sacrifice,*
> *A Holy Spirit's energies,*
> *An advocate with God.*

nature; he had to forego that knowledge. For not only did he *bear* our sin for us, but he was *made sin* for us:

*God made him who had no sin to be sin for us,
so that in him we might become the righteousness of God. (2 Corinthians 5:21)*

Of all the descriptions of the Atonement in scripture, this is surely one of the most graphic. It comes at the close of perhaps the most profound exposition ever of suffering and glory in the whole of 2 Corinthians 4 & 5. It is just not possible to skate onto the next chapter without a deep sense of wonder at the depth of Christ's love.

Fierce, costly love

In Gethsemane Jesus turned to his disciples in his very human suffering seeking human solace.[15] As the Psalmist had written: 'Scorn has broken my heart and has left me helpless; I looked for sympathy, but there was none, for comforters, but I found none.'[16] How much the memory of Mary of Bethany's anointing must have meant to him. Evidently she understood. On Calvary as the Son of God lost the last consciousness of his Father's love and presence, our forgiveness would be won.

In the Lord's final words in the Garden he tells his disciples to sleep on, then seems immediately to ask them to wake up as it is time to leave.[17] We can assume that some hours passed in between; hours in which Christ sat watching over them as they slept. What a picture of love when he was in need.

As the Psalmist wrote, 'He who watches over Israel will neither slumber nor sleep'.[18] It is a strangely peaceful scene as Christ thinks thoughts of love beyond human expression—fierce, costly love—revealing the longing heart of God. This is the message of Gethsemane. And this was the scene on which Judas arrived, accompanied by the Roman soldiers who would arrest Jesus.

JESUS ON TRIAL

Jesus was taken first to Ananias, father-in-law of Caiaphas the high priest, then to Caiaphas, then to Pilate the following morning. Pilate passed him on to Herod, and Herod back to Pilate for sentence. He was tried by both Church and State. The Jews wanted to crucify Jesus on religious grounds but they had no power, as a nation subject to Rome, to sentence anyone to death; only the Romans could do this, and in Roman law blasphemy was not an indictable offence. This is why the Jews had to charge him with treason as well as with blasphemy; to do this they cunningly portrayed his claim to be a king as an act of treason.

JESUS REMAINED SILENT

Christ submitted to injustice. He could have out-argued his accusers in pleading his case. Yet, as a sheep before her shearers is silent, so he did not open his mouth. Jesus took on himself the guilt of the world's sin, and guilt silences us. He had nothing to say, because there is nothing to say before a holy God. He could have defended himself but he did not. He *chose* to be found guilty, to stand in for us.[19]

What a contrast with Paul's triumphant climax in Romans 8:31–38. Because of Christ's death and resurrection the Apostle can ask, 'If God is for us, who can be against us?' for 'Who will bring any charge against those whom God has chosen?' Who indeed, if the charges against us are laid on him? 'Who is he that condemns?' Who indeed, if Christ who died for us, and has been raised from the dead, is at the right hand of God, praying for us? This is why the Apostle Paul declares us 'more than conquerors' and why 'neither death nor life . . . nor anything in all creation will be able to separate us from the love of God that is in Christ Jesus our Lord.'

The trial was a shameful farce, unjust and illegal. It was hurried; it was held at the wrong time; it was unlawfully confirmed; and the chief priests and the whole Sanhedrin deliberately sought out witnesses to bring false evidence. But is this surprising? No true court of justice could have secured a conviction against the sinless Christ. Notice how God's sovereign purpose is serenely at work; he actually uses the designs of human evil to fulfil his wonderful eternal purpose in bringing salvation (Acts 4:27–28).

But why a trial at all? Was it only a pretext to get rid of Jesus? Why not hire a hitman, or arrange a secret poisoning? Surely this would have achieved the same result? But God decreed otherwise. As Christ stood on trial in our place, these particular charges had to be brought. In Revelation 20:11–15 we see the great white throne at the final judgment; here the books are opened. This is the trial which awaits all who have not put their trust in Jesus Christ, as their substitute and sin-bearer, all whose names are not written in the Lamb's Book of Life. The two charges against Christ, blasphemy and treason, are the very charges against the whole human race. In every sense, he stood in for us, and bore what was ours, and gave us what was his.

All four gospel writers record Pilate's words that he could find no charge against him. Yet emotion was running high in the crowd and a riot could break out if Christ were not found guilty.

Should Pilate let Christ go free? In his terrible dilemma he passed the decision to the crowd; they could choose between Christ and Barabbas, another man listed for crucifixion that day. Barabbas was a robber and an insurrectionist who had led a revolt against Rome, and was in prison awaiting execution. He knew he deserved to die. The crowd chose Barabbas, and Christ died in his place that afternoon, the just for the unjust. There is a kind of parable in the story of Barabbas. His name means literally 'son of his father'. He could be any one of us.

THE JUST FOR THE UNJUST

'Christ died for sins once for all, the righteous for the unrighteous, to bring you to God.' 1 Peter 3:18

This verse is the anchor to which Peter attaches most of his first letter, and it evidently occupies his thoughts.

We rightly speak of the love of God when we think of the gospel; it was God the Father's love that sent Christ to be the Saviour of the world, but it was ultimately justice that atoned for sin. This is Peter's point, and Paul, too, gives priority to it. Paul was proud of the gospel of Christ (Romans 1:16) not because it was an expression of the divine love—although that is certainly true—but because the righteousness of God is revealed in it. We see the same emphasis in John's writing. In his first letter he declared that 'God is faithful and just to forgive us our sins and to cleanse us from all un-righteousness.'

Priests and Prophets

We read at the opening of the letter to the Hebrews, 'In the past God spoke to our forefathers through the prophets at many times and in various ways, but in these last days he has spoken to us by his Son.' So there were different strands of revelation through the Old Testament, none complete in itself, but each pointing beyond itself, and finally culminating in Christ. This is how God gradually revealed himself to people.

In the Old Testament we trace two great attempts at solving the problem of sin, both inspired by God, each complementary to the other, and both finding their fruition in Christ. These were the priestly system and prophetic ministry.

Priests: The Old Testament sacrificial system was elaborately intricate, but its message may be summed up like this:

Sacrifice is the remedy for sin, and 'without the shedding of blood there is no forgiveness' (Hebrews 9:22). Christ's death fulfilled this sacrifice but more than that, he himself became our High Priest (Hebrews 2:17) so no more sacrifices would ever be needed.

Prophets: People multiplied their sacrifices, but their hearts remained far from God.

And so God in his continuing mercy sent prophets, and the supreme note in prophetic preaching is ethical. The prophets called for a change of heart. 'What does the Lord require of you? To act justly, and to love mercy, and to walk humbly with your God' (Micah 6:8). But this is a counsel of despair, for it is beyond our capability as sinners whose natural orientation, as we know all too well, is to pride and selfishness.

So where does this leave us with our natural inclination to sin? The priestly and the prophetic systems both offered only temporary solutions, interim answers to this problem. The blood of bulls and of goats could not take away sin. And prophetic witness could not produce in people's hearts what was demanded. There is only one effective solution. The wonderful good news of the gospel is that the prophetic and priestly systems are both fulfilled, and indeed meet, in Christ.

Micah's words may not be known by our unbelieving friends, neighbours or colleagues, nor may these people have any knowledge of the meaning of Christ's death, but they *will* be aware of having done wrong, and of having let others down; and they will sense a need for forgiveness. We are all people with a past, and that can bring regret, and even fear. How to repair the past is one of the great universal questions. Until our past is dealt with, there can be no possibility of a relationship with God. For all our longing, we ourselves cannot repair the past.

Longing to repair the past

The Persian mathematician and poet Omar Khayya'm, who lived a thousand years ago, wrote:

*'The moving finger writes, and having writ
    moves on;
Nor all thy piety nor wit can lure it back to
    cancel half a line,
Nor all thy tears wash out a word of it.'* [20]

This yearning is universal and has been a constant theme and thread of world literature down the centuries. The regrets and the 'if onlys' taunt us. We can put our past failures out of our minds, but if they are not repented of then eventually, maybe even years later, they return, and we find ourselves greatly troubled by them until we come to Christ in repentance and ask his forgiveness. Then we have peace. Deep down we know right from wrong.

Lady Macbeth desperately tries to wash the blood stain from her hands after the death of King Duncan, yet it will not disappear. 'Out, out damned spot. Out, I say!' we hear her cry, as she wanders around during the night.[21] She cannot escape her guilt through sleep; it engulfs her.

Briony Tallis in Ian McEwan's *Atonement* invested her life in trying to make good a foolish action at the age of thirteen. Her book, *Atone-*

ment, took her fifty-nine years to complete. Now she has vascular dementia and is dying. Briony longs that she could rewrite history. (She does in a sense, but only as a novelist.) She wants to give a happy ending to her sister, who had died many years before; to give her sister the happy life which she had denied her. But Briony knows that writing a novel cannot achieve atonement.[22] Atonement can come only from beyond ourselves.

Briony's shrewd perception, her gift in writing, and her imagination are all she has, and they are beginning to fail her.

Briony, Lady Macbeth, Omar: come with us into the gospel records. Hear Christ's call to all who are weary and burdened. 'I am gentle and humble in heart' says the Lord Jesus, 'and you will find rest for your souls'.[23]

God wants his picture back

The sacrificial system addressed the negative aspect of the problem, the penalty of sin; the prophetic system speaks of the positive, atoning element. Let us look at how these two work together. Suppose a painting is stolen from a private collection. The police track down the thief who is sent for trial, found guilty, and put in prison. The penalty is exacted for his crime. But this does not put matters right. The art collector says, 'I want my picture back'. And only when it is returned can the matter rest. For full atonement two things are involved: the punishment of the crime and the repair of the injury.

Christ paid the penalty for our sin, but God, as it were, wants *his* picture back—the image of himself in human beings, before that image became marred by sin. In Christ's life of grace and beauty, God had the picture returned. Full atonement.

This double aspect of Christ's atoning work is captured so memorably by the hymnwriter Philip Bliss:

> *Bearing shame and scoffing rude,*
> *In my place condemned he stood,*
> *Sealed my pardon with his blood.*
> *Hallelujah, what a Saviour!*
>
> *Guilty vile and helpless we;*
> *Spotless Lamb of God was he:*
> Full atonement—*can it be?*
> *Hallelujah, what a Saviour!*

WHY HAVE YOU FORSAKEN ME?

In Christ's cry from the cross, 'My God, my God, why have you forsaken me?' we see the biblical idea of substitution. There was no answer to that terrible cry; God was silent. Christ had been silent in his trial, having no defence to offer, with the weight of our sin on his shoulders. Now there is silence from heaven. There could be no answer from God; for that is what hell means. And in the terrible agony of that silence, atonement was made and our forgiveness was sealed in blood.

JUSTIFICATION AND SACRIFICE

We may not *feel* guilty but the Scriptures speak of our guilt before God as an objective reality (Romans 3:19, 20). Some people have less sensitive consciences than others, but how we feel does not change how God sees us.

Guilt is an objective reality. Justification, which deals with it, is also objective. It is something God does; it is a declaration God makes about us. It is, as the 17th century Shorter Catechism of the Church of Scotland says, 'an act of God's free grace, in which he, the Judge of all the earth, acquits the guilty sinner, and declares him to be righteous, and accepts him as righteous in his sight.'[24]

The Greek word translated 'justify' (*dikaioun*) means 'to count, or treat, as righteous', not to make righteous in any ethical sense. Justification is not something that is done *in* us, but something done *to* us and *for* us, and *outside* us. This is made possible only because of the death of Jesus Christ as our substitute, in our place.

In the early chapters of Romans, Paul is comparing two scenarios. The first is a sombre and dark depiction of human beings; the image in which we were created has been marred; we are now a travesty, a caricature of what God had planned. But Jesus Christ as 'the second Adam' is all that we are not.

Let's not miss the sheer drama of the comparison. On the one hand we have 'the many'—humankind as a whole, in the first Adam—guilty before God; on the other hand we have 'the One' who is perfect.

Christ came to substitute his humanity, in all its excellence and perfection, for our sinfulness. Nothing about us is acceptable to God. From our conception, we have all been sinners (see Psalms 51 and 139).

Christ identifies with us from that very point: he was conceived by the Holy Spirit and born for us; he was baptized for us; he was tempted for us; he lived for us; he stood trial for us, taking on himself the charges that were against us; he suffered and died for us, going into the outer darkness for our sakes; and he rose again for us.[25]

All his 'work' is imputed to us—counted as if it were ours—in his death on the cross, and our sin is counted as if it were his. It is this divine exchange that lies at the heart of the gospel, and makes it a gospel.

Charles Wesley's hymn 'And can it be' sums it up:

No condemnation now I dread;
Jesus, and all in him, is mine!
Alive in him, my living Head,
And clothed in righteousness divine,
Bold I approach the eternal throne,
And claim the crown, through Christ my own.

The prophet Zechariah gives a graphic picture of this great exchange in one of the earlier visions of his prophecy (Zechariah 3:1–5). Joshua the high priest appears before the angel of the Lord, with Satan ready to accuse him. The Lord rebukes Satan, and speaks of Joshua as a burning stick snatched from the fire. Zechariah continues:

> 'Now Joshua was dressed in filthy clothes as he stood before the angel. Then the angel said to those who were standing before him, "Take off his filthy clothes." Then he said to Joshua, "See, I have taken away your sin, and I will put rich garments on you." And I said, "Put a clean turban on his head." So they set a clean turban on his head, and clothed him while the angel of the LORD stood by.'

As we have already seen, the great themes of the gospel permeate the Scriptures and are threaded through them, each passage adding more light and texture. Martin Luther, reflecting on this theme in Romans wrote: 'I greatly longed to understand Paul's epistle to the Romans, but one expression stood in my way, namely "the righteousness of God". I took it to mean that God is righteous and deals righteously in punishing the unrighteous.' He goes on to explain how he suddenly realised the context of these words; that righteousness is a gift received by faith. The very words which had been so hard to understand now became 'inexpressibly sweet'.[26] Luther's discovery of the meaning of the Atonement sparked the sixteenth century Protestant Reformation.

The sacrifice itself

No metaphor is perfect. The law court metaphor is helpful in illustrating our needs, but it does not deal with God's 'needs'. And by its nature it has something impersonal about it. The human judge in any court of law, in his official capacity, is an impartial figure. His job is simply to administer justice, and to see it is administered fairly. He is not angry with the accused; the trial is all in a day's work. He can go home in the evening and forget about the whole thing. But God cannot forget. He cannot brush sin aside as if it had not happened.

God has been made angry by sin, and this presents a serious problem.

God's anger is turned away by the sacrifice of Christ on the cross. This does not suggest, as some would have it, that God is a bloodthirsty, vengeful deity.[27] Nor does it contradict all we read of a loving God.

We are powerless to do anything about our sin. At infinite cost to himself, God in Christ took our punishment *in his own person*, in our place. 'This is love, not that we loved God, but that he loved us, and sent his Son to be the propitiation for our sins' (1 John 4:10).[28] What love!

AN IMPORTANT DISTINCTION

The theological terms 'propitiation' and 'penal substitution' refer to the fact that Christ bore our punishment for us, in our place, to appease the wrath of God. This doctrine has come under attack at certain periods in church history, and again in recent years. Some Bible translators prefer to translate the Greek word *hilasmos* (used in 1 John 2:2 and 1 John 4:10) as 'expiation', which I believe is inadequate. Expiation emphasizes the payment of a penalty, but contains no sense of the need to appease a holy God.

The eternal God found his peace—his appeasement from righteous anger—at the cross. This is the meaning of the term 'propitiation'.

As human anger is usually wrong, we tend to think that anger from God must also be wrong. But love and wrath are not contradictory. God does not stop loving us although he is angry with us for our sin, any more than a parent stops loving his child when the child has done wrong.

It is holiness, not punishment of sin, which pleases God. The seriousness of the situation, in God's sight, comes home to us when we consider his character. Let me quote again from the Shorter Catechism. The language may be old, but it is full of profound truth:

'God is a Spirit, infinite, eternal, unchangeable, in his being, wisdom, power, holiness, justice, goodness and truth.' Justice and judgment are the habitation of his throne, clouds and darkness overshadow him. He is the Father of an infinite majesty; jealous, omnipotent, holy, terrible. He is of purer eyes than to behold evil, he cannot look on iniquity.

So long as the relationship between humankind and God remains broken, there can be no thought of peace with God. Atonement comes only at the cross. To quote Horatius Bonar, a great Scottish hymnwriter:

> I hear the words of love,
> I gaze upon the blood,
> I see the mighty Sacrifice,
> And I have peace with God.

Let us pause here, or we may miss something. The precious blood of Christ brings peace not only to sinful, guilty human hearts, but also to the holy heart of God. As he gazes upon the blood, and sees the mighty Sacrifice, he too enters into peace.

OUR WONDERFUL
REDEMPTION

Let's now look at three pictures which show different aspects of God's plan of redemption.

The *first* picture is that of finding the lost sheep in Luke 15:1–7. It is such a telling image. The shepherd loves each sheep so much that he will take the risk of leaving the ninety-nine to go in search of the one which is lost. But there is another vital aspect to the story. The lost sheep is powerless to find his way, and he needs the shepherd to come and look for him.

The *second* picture is that of defeating the enemy, in his struggle for power. Again, we cannot do anything ourselves. God, in Christ, delivers us, transferring us out of the kingdom of darkness and into the kingdom of his dear Son (Colossians 1:13, 2:11–15).

The *third* picture is that of our redemption. The same word 'redeem' was used in Israel's deliverance from Egypt. 'I am the LORD your God, who brought you out of Egypt, out of the land of slavery.' Christ's redeeming blood takes the place of the Passover lamb; it brings us into a new covenant relationship with God.

Paul expounds this new covenant in detail in Romans 6–8, three wonderfully rich chapters looking at the theme of our union with Christ in his death and resurrection.

Two kinds of faith

It is by faith alone that we receive God's grace in the gospel. This word is used in two ways. Propositional faith means to 'believe that he exists, and that he rewards those who earnestly seek him' (Hebrews 11:6). But to have faith in Christ also refers to our placing personal trust in him. The two complement each other, and neither can stand alone. When a person has only propositional faith without exercising a true and personal trust, there is a danger signal.

Faith as personal trust is prominent in Paul's thinking. He yearns that the early Christians be grounded thoroughly in doctrine because truth sets the heart on fire. His own love of the Saviour is clearly evident in his writing and in the way he prayed. He trusted Christ in a vital and intimate way, and he would have been very familiar with the Old Testament Hebrew words all rendered as 'trust' in the English versions. The most frequently-used are:

> *galal*—to roll upon, in the sense of rolling a
>   burden upon another

chul—to rely on, with the idea of trusting in
the dark

chasah—to take refuge in

batach—to lean upon, in helplessness and
weakness

FAITH GROUNDED ON TRUTH

Justification, propitiation and redemption can
hardly be separated in our experience, though
we must distinguish them in thought. The
verdict of guilty puts the criminal in prison; if
he is acquitted, he is set free. But when we are
acquitted in God's eyes (justified) through the
blood of Christ (the propitiatory sacrifice) we
are not simply declared righteous in an objective sense, but we are given power through the
Holy Spirit of Christ living in us.

We cannot understand Paul's teaching on justification, propitiation and redemption if we
do not grasp Paul's teaching on propositional
truth. Something happened on the cross at
Calvary; the possibility of a new relationship
was established between the eternal creator
God and human beings. That is objective fact;
it does not rest on our spiritual experience.
This is the truth on which our personal faith
is grounded.

Each carries a strong suggestion of help-lessness; these words would have been at the forefront of Paul the pastor's thinking; they underlie all he taught in Romans about our helpless predicament.

We must also remember faith is the gift of God to those who believe, and that it comes through hearing the truth explained.[29] It is when people listen to the message of the gospel, and understand it, that they begin to make new discoveries about Christ, and glimpse something of his wonder and his greatness.

THE GLORY OF THE CROSS

Christ prayed for himself in the Garden: 'And now, Father, glorify me in your presence with the glory I had with you before the world began' (John 17:5). This Christ who lives in us by his Spirit is the glorified Christ, glorified through his death.

Only one response from us is possible, a response of worship. The chorus of Bob Kauflin's hymn uses the Apostle Paul's words (see Philippians 1:7–11) to express this.

And, oh, the glory of the cross
That you would send your Son for us;
I gladly count my life as loss
That I might come to know
The glory of, the glory of the cross.[30]

The cross and evangelism

The whole of 2 Corinthians 4 & 5 is one of the richest theological passages in the New Testament. It says so much about the gospel that it is difficult to know where to begin, and it is impossible to exhaust all its truth. We have looked at the narrative accounts of Christ's death in the gospels, and have traced back what we called 'the trajectory of grace' from the Passover. Now we look at the implications for ourselves in that trajectory, as those who have died and been raised with Christ.

In 2 Corinthians 5 we see the love of Christ in the death that he died; the reconciliation achieved in that death; and how we become new creations when we hear and receive the great invitation. Then comes our wonderful commission by God himself to preach the reconciling word.

The word 'reconciliation' is used five times in 2 Corinthians 5: twice of God's reconciling work in Christ, twice of the ministry he has committed to us, and once in the exhortation made in the gospel, 'Be reconciled to God'. Reconciliation is central to our message.

If we are gripped by the truth of the gospel, we find ourselves compelled to tell others. What a privilege beyond imagination that we should be Christ's ambassadors, as though God were making his appeal through us (2 Corinthians 5:20). First century ambassadors were sometimes mistreated or even imprisoned by those to whom they were sent. However these incidents were always condemned, as we learn from the historian Livy; but not so with Christ's ambassadors, either then or now. Paul is truly Christ's ambassador. He is preaching the gospel in the spirit of the gospel, and pleads with his readers to be reconciled to God. This is how we too are to exercise our role as ambassadors; and in this we too follow the example of Christ himself. For, as we have already reminded ourselves, the Lord says, 'Come to me', as he longingly invites us to receive the gift of life. He is a humble God.[31]

The verb used in some translations in 2 Corinthians 5:14 is not 'compels' (as in the NIV) but 'constrains'. Paul is using the metaphor of a horse. Christ's love 'held him in' in the way a rein 'holds in' a horse so that it can be given true direction under the skilful hand of its rider. This is how the horse is made to give of its very best. The rider brings out every latent power, drawing an unruly spirit under submission. So it is with Christ's followers. The constraint of divine love brings our thoughts and our energy into submission to Christ. And as the Apostle Paul writes, his mind unerringly goes to the mystery of Christ's death, to what was achieved on the cross, and to the miracle of the new creation. This is where the constraint of Christ's love led him! It was the same for all the apostles as they preached the risen and ascended Christ, and it should be the same for us. Such is the glory of the cross.

A close-up view of Calvary

Christ 'became obedient to death—even death on a cross!' (Philippians 2:8). As we have seen, our Lord chose to die, and that choice was in obedience to God's will. He remained silent when he could have confounded his accusers; he would not come down from the cross when he could have called on twelve legions of angels to deliver him. It was not the nails, but sheer love, and obedience to the Father's will, that kept him hanging there: love and obedience, in spite of temptations to take an easier way—even when his grasp of eternal reality became clouded.

This voluntary obedience gives the Atonement its moral value, and here we see Christ as the great example. 'Your attitude should be the same as Christ Jesus, who became obedient to death—even death on a cross.'[33]

Christ has 'destroyed death, and has brought life and immortality to light through the gospel' (2 Timothy 1:10). The word translated 'destroyed' means 'to bring to nothing'. The idea is that death has been overcome or vanquished through the gospel. Christ's death, then, was a victory over death.

Let us pause to look at this carefully.

Death is the great enemy to be dealt with; one could call it the 'sacrament' of sin.[34] Through Adam and Eve, death 'reigned' in human experience (Romans 5:14, 21). To establish instead a reign of grace and life, a battle with death would be needed.

Already Christ had had skirmishes with the power of death—in the raising of Jairus' daughter,

DEATH IN ITS HIDEOUS INTENSITY

The early Church was taught in detail about Christ's death; it remained its driving force and inspiration, as we see from New Testament writing. The writer to the Hebrews states that Christ 'tasted death for everyone'. He tasted not merely physical cessation of life, but death in its hideous intensity and power, such as no one has known or can know.[32]

the widow of Nain's son, and Lazarus. But now came the decisive battle. There was no other way for death to be dealt with decisively; Christ himself, the Prince and Lord of all life, needed to destroy it from the inside. This is the great crescendo of the gospel record. Jesus is Lord over disease, Lord over devils, Lord over nature and Lord of people like us—it was not possible that death should hold him!

Now we see, in stark simplicity, how the drama and mystery of Jesus's death is actually felt and experienced by those who were there at the time. The darkness which fell over the whole earth as he was dying was symbolic of the darkness that is outside the gates of God, and of the nameless horror of eternal loss.

Matthew tells us that in the moment he died 'the curtain in the temple was torn in two, from the top to the bottom' (Matthew 27:51). The curtain separated the Holy Place in the temple from the holiest of all, the inmost sanctuary.[35] In Old Testament times, this was where the presence of the Lord dwelt. No one was allowed to enter apart from the high priest, and that only once a year, on the Day of Atonement, to make atonement for the sins of the people. The curtain was the 'sign' that there was no way into the divine presence. It was like the shut gate of the Garden of Eden. The way to God had been barred by sin. The torn curtain declared that Christ has opened up the way home to God.

Matthew goes on to describe how the earth shook, tombs broke open, and people of faith who had died were raised to life (Matthew 27:51ff). These verses are often taken as no more than a pious legend; people feel they cannot be true as these things could not have happened. But it was an extraordinary time and something very extraordinary was taking place. God was in Christ reconciling the world to himself—that is how big a thing was happening! Is it surprising that there should have been dislocations in the natural order? This moment is of cosmic importance.

Jesus was crucified because the rulers did not believe his claim to be the Son of God. This claim was clearly bandied about in the judgment hall and at Calvary, as Christ became the subject of mockery, and the soldiers joined in the general shouting of 'Hail, king of the Jews'. But then these hardened men had to take him and nail him to the cross. They had never seen such a prisoner, nor had they ever seen such a death as his, accompanied by such fearful signs.

Matthew tells of the centurion in charge of the soldiers who crucified Jesus (Matthew 27:54). Think of him: a Roman, perhaps a hardened soldier. That Friday started for him as just another day, but it ended very differently. When the centurion saw all this, he became convinced that Christ must be what he claimed to be. Spiritual light had dawned. His words give a foretaste of a great movement down the centuries and across the nations as people are drawn to faith, and say as he said: 'Truly this was the Son of God'.

The gospel transcends cultures and political divisions; it is for all, paying no regard to education or to wealth. What was true of the centurion that afternoon is also true of Joseph of Arimathea (Matthew 27:57–60). There could be no greater contrast between these two men: one a rough soldier, the other a rich Pharisee and counsellor of the Jews—yet at the cross they are both on the same level, and both found salvation.

We are told that Joseph was Jesus' disciple, but John adds a significant comment in his record (John 19:38), 'but secretly, for fear of the Jews'. The cross drew him out into the open, to declare his allegiance.

Nicodemus helped Joseph of Arimathea to wrap the Lord's body and lay him in the tomb. He had earlier come to seek out Jesus at night. Nicodemus had not clearly understood Christ's teaching when we meet him in John 3, but he was slowly drawn into the light as he continued his quest for truth (John 7:50,51). Now, at the cross, he too takes a clear stand as Christ's disciple.

The cross will always divide. It is a stumbling block to the Jews. Hearing of a crucified Saviour, now raised to life, drew scoffing from among the Athenians gathered to listen to Paul at Mars Hill. But the cross must never be left out of our gospel message in the hope of making it more attractive. Without the cross there would be no gospel. Indeed as Christians we must all bear the mark of the cross in our lives as those who have died with Christ, and been raised with him to serve him in humility.

Christians have been helped in worship for three hundred years by singing Isaac Watts's searching hymn, 'When I survey the wondrous cross' and it brings our reflection to a fitting close. Here is the true perspective, the Apostle Paul's perspective. Let it be ours as the cross leaves its imprint on our lives and our ambitions, and on our fellowship with other Christians, and with the Saviour himself.

When I survey the wondrous cross
On which the Prince of Glory died,
My richest gain I count but loss
And pour contempt on all my pride.

Forbid it, Lord, that I should boast
Save in the cross of Christ my God;
The very things that charm me most—
I sacrifice them to his blood.

See from his head, his hands, his feet,
Sorrow and love flow mingled down:
When did such love and sorrow meet,
Or thorns compose so rich a crown?

Were the whole realm of nature mine,
That were an offering far too small;
Love so amazing, so divine
Demands my soul, my life, my all.

Isaac Watts (1674–1748)

Hallelujah! What a Saviour!

JESUS WILL RETURN

Since its first publication, this title has been read by many people who are not yet Christians. So we decided to add a postscript to newer editions, as not all readers have heard what happened next.

Christ died carrying the weight of the sin of the whole world. But death could not hold him, for he was, and is, the eternal Son of God, who had no sin. On the first Easter Sunday morning, when Mary Magdalene and other women went to the tomb where his body had been laid, they were shocked at what they discovered. The stone covering its entrance had been rolled away; the tomb was empty. God had raised Christ from the dead.

The end of the New Testament gospel narratives and the Book of Acts give marvellous accounts of the way Christ appeared to his disciples, walked, talked and ate with them; and the Apostle Paul writes of how he was seen by many others. After 40 days he ascended to heaven.

Now he sits at God's right hand, where he is praying for us. One day he will return to earth, not as he first came, born in a stable, but in glory.

To find out more, talk with a Christian friend, or join local Christians for Sunday worship.

Many churches now offer midweek courses for people to explore the Christian faith at their own pace. You will find some listed on www.christianityexplored.org.

There are now more Christians in more countries than there have ever been in the history of the church. We trust you have been helped to grasp the meaning of Christ's death, and that you, too, will find faith in him.

FOR STUDY AND REFLECTION

- Take time for an unhurried read through the synoptic gospels, and then through John's gospel. The same Lord Jesus, his work finished, is now interceding for us in all our human struggles (Hebrews 4:14–5:9). What new things have you learned about his humanity as we have walked through his last day on earth?

- We don't know whether Barabbas was among the crowd that terrible Friday afternoon, but it is very possible he was there. I wonder if he came to faith as he reflected on Jesus dying—quite literally—in his place. We are told that one of the thieves found faith then (Luke 23:39–43). Sometimes we can dismiss people as not worth sharing the gospel with. What do we learn from Jesus's words to the thief?

- From Genesis 3 onwards, people have been searching for something to ease the conscience and give peace, something to deal with a guilty past. It's important to recognise that this searching in our hearts is God-given and God-inspired (Acts 17:26ff; Ecclesiastes 3:11); this should bring great confidence in sharing the gospel, and a sense of expectation as we do so. How can we help our friends, family, colleagues to find peace? What opportunities do books and films like *Atonement* and *The Kite Runner* give us?

- Read Romans 3:21–26. Here are all the great themes of the gospel in microcosm. The words righteousness, justification, propitiation, redemption and faith each have a specific and precise meaning, all contributing to the full picture. With the help of a Bible dictionary or, for example, J I Packer's *18 Words* (Christian Focus Publications), trace these themes through Paul's letters to gain a good grasp of the rich meaning of each of them.

- 2 Corinthians 4 & 5 are filled with profound commentary on the theme of suffering and glory. Here the Apostle Paul opens out the wonder and mystery of God's plan for our salvation. Read the chapters slowly and let them seep into your thinking, and your praying. I never tire of their sheer depth and beauty. You may like to learn them by heart—then they can feed your thinking as you travel to work, or go for a walk, or do the gardening etc.

- We are to remember Christ's death until he returns in glory. As we share bread and wine in church, we 'proclaim' his death (1 Corinthians 11:26), rehearsing God's promise to act justly to forgive our sins as we come in repentance (1 John 1:7,9). The Apostle Paul wrote movingly to the Galatians 'he loved me and gave himself for me' (Galatians 2:20). Take time to worship him quietly on your own for dying for you.

- What marks identify a growing Christian? Look at the recommended reading on 'union with Christ' (p38) and work through one of the books listed, or another which deals with this area. Our union with him is surely the richest aspect of the Christian life, and one which will always take us deeper, and higher, and onward.

NOTES

1. It is worth giving time to a study of the Passover and its foreshadowing of the Cross. John Stott's *The Cross of Christ* (see recommended reading p38) addresses this in more detail than can be included here.

2. Note how Matthew and Mark record the Lord Jesus as saying that his blood was shed 'for many' (Matthew 26:28; Mark 14:24) and Luke 'for you' (Luke 22:20). He evidently said both. Even in the intimacy of the communion service as we remember Christ's death for our sakes, the Lord Jesus directs our eyes and our hearts to those who are not yet within the covenant. He is a missionary God.

3. The Apostle Paul described union with Christ very simply in Philippians 1:21: 'For to me, to live is Christ'. Our union with him is the essence of the Christian life. For further reading see p38.

4. See 1 John 1:3b; John 15:15

5. The Apostle Paul is a great model for us here. He has given us the basis for our New Testament theology, all written and preached with a passion for Christ, whom he loved dearly. He longed for Christians to understand what it means to 'live by faith in the Son of God'. Paul knew nothing of 'arid' doctrine. Doctrinal truth set his heart on fire.

6. The gospels of Matthew, Mark and Luke are often referred to as 'the synoptic gospels'. There is a sense in which they portray the life, death and resurrection of Christ from the same point of view; John brings a different perspective.

7. This makes sense of his choice to omit the account of Christ's transfiguration, found in all the synoptic gospels.

8. John 18:1–4; Luke 22:39

9. New Testament writers had a deep sense of symbolism. Gethsemane had earlier associations. In the story of the revolt of David's son Absalom (2 Samuel 15:30), David wept on Mount Olivet, the same place where his 'greater Son' now faced a greater revolt, that of the human race against the true and living God. David had company in his grief; Jesus was alone. 'Gethsemane' literally means 'an oil-press' or 'winepress', and in Jesus' day the Garden was a grove of olives with a winepress. The Gethsemane experience was for Christ the beginning of the action of the wine-press of God. 'I have trodden the winepress alone; from the nations no-one was with me' (Isaiah 63:3). Even his inner circle, Peter, James and John, could not penetrate his awesome loneliness.

10. Hebrews 4:15

11. Luke 4:13. See also Peter's appeal in Matthew 16:22–23; Mark 8:31–33

12. The writer to the Hebrews (Hebrews 5:7–10) speaks of Christ praying with 'loud cries and tears'. This reference is clearly to Gethsemane. What was 'heard' (v7) was not 'May this cup be taken from me'— for that was not granted—but rather 'not as I will but as you will.' His cry was for strength to go through with what he knew to be the Father's will. And we see his prayer answered in the calm serenity which rested upon him right through to the crucifixion itself.

13. See Matthew 26:37–38; Mark 14:33–34

14. John 18:11

15. Matthew 26:40, 43

16. Psalm 69:20

17. Matthew 26:45–46

18. Psalm 121:4

19. See Matthew 26:53; Isaiah 53:7–12; Romans 3:19

20. Omar Khayya'm lived from 1048–1131. I quote from Edward Fitzgerald's 19th century translation of *The Ruba'iya't*.

21. Shakespeare's *Macbeth*. Act 5, Scene 1: lines 26–40

22. 'The problem these fifty-nine years has been this: how can a novelist achieve atonement, when, with her absolute power of deciding outcomes, she is also God? There is no one, no entity or higher form that she can appeal to, or be reconciled with, or that can forgive her. There is nothing outside her. In her imagination she has set the limits and the terms. No atonement for God, or novelists, even if they are atheists. It was always an impossible task, and that was precisely the point. The attempt was all.' Ian McEwan, *Atonement* p371

23. Matthew 11:28,29

24. The Shorter Catechism was drawn up in 1647, as a question-and-answer means of training church members in the Christian faith. It was one of the major documents to come out of the Reformation.

25. Christ knew us before even our conception, for we were chosen in him before the foundation of the world (see for example Ephesians 1). He is our Saviour in time and in eternity.

26. Martin Luther, *Preface to Latin Writings*, 1545, 34, p337

27. See Steve Jeffery, Mike Ovey, Andrew Sach: *Pierced for our Transgressions* (IVP 2007) for a full and helpful defence of this argument.

28. The NIV does not use the word 'propitiation' here, yet it is clear in the Greek.

29. Philippians 1:29; Romans 10:17

30. Bob Kauflin, 'The Glory of the Cross' from 'Songs of the Cross-Centered Life', Sovereign Grace Music, 2000

31. Lindsay Brown gives a wonderful contemporary example of Christ's humility in the opening chapter of *Shining Like Stars: the power of the gospel in the world's universities* (IVP). He reflects on the irony that 'the one in whom are hidden all the treasures of wisdom and knowledge' should be held in disregard or derision in the world's universities, the very places where wisdom and knowledge are deemed to be sought and taught. The university is arguably the most influential institution (in human terms) in any nation. Islam has a well-funded plan to place academics and administrators in strategic positions in academia, but in many of the world's universities the only ambassadors of the humble Christ are students, young in the faith, holding out the word of life to their friends and to faculty.

32. It is interesting to note the contrast of expressions used in the New Testament. Lazarus and Jairus' daughter are described as 'sleeping' but Jesus 'died'.

33. See Philippians 2:3–11

34. The reason that physical death is so sinister is because of the spiritual death which lies behind it.

35. According to the Roman historian Josephus, this curtain was gigantic, some 80 feet high. It was, he says, a 'Babylonian tapestry, with embroidery of blue

and fine linen, of scarlet also and purple, wrought
with marvellous skill. Nor was this mixture of mate-
rials without its mystic meaning: it typified the uni-
verse. Portrayed on this tapestry was a panorama of
the entire heavens.' David Ulansey in the *Journal of
Biblical Literature* 110:1 (Spring 1991) pp 123–25

RECOMMENDED READING

On the Cross

The Cross of Christ by John Stott (IVP)
Cross Examined by Mark Meynell (IVP)
The Gospel and the Achievement of the Cross by
    Mark Chan (Lausanne)
Living the Cross-Centered Life by C J Mahaney
    (Multnomah)

On Union with Christ

The Growing Christian by James Philip (Christian
    Focus Publications)
The Holy Spirit by Sinclair Ferguson (IVP)
Book III, *Institutes of the Christian Religion* by
    John Calvin (several)

The James Philip digital library

James Philip's preaching through the whole
Bible, and his daily reading notes, may be found
at www.thetron.org

From the Lausanne Movement

The Cape Town Commitment: A Call to Action. A Study Guide for Small Groups. Compiled by Sara Singleton and Matt Ristuccia (Hendrickson Publishers)

The Cape Town Commitment: Study Edition. A Confession of Faith and a Call to Action by Rose Dowsett (Hendrickson Publishers)

Ephesians: Studying with the Global Church by Lindsay Olesberg. Participant's Guide (Hendrickson Publishers)

Creation Care and the Gospel. Lausanne Consult 1. Edited by Colin Bell and Robert S White (Hendrickson Publishers)

The Grace of Giving: Money and the Gospel (Hendrickson Publishers)

Lausanne Movement

Connecting influencers and ideas for global mission

The Lausanne Movement takes its name from the International Congress on World Evangelization, convened in 1974 in Lausanne, Switzerland, by the US evangelist Billy Graham. His long-time friend John Stott, the UK pastor-theologian, was chief architect of *The Lausanne Covenant*, which issued from this gathering.

Two further global Congresses followed— the second in Manila, Philippines (1989) and the third in Cape Town, South Africa (2010). From the Third Lausanne Congress came *The Cape Town Commitment: A Confession of Faith and a Call to Action*. Its Call to Action was the fruit of a careful process conducted over four years to discern what we believe the Holy Spirit is saying to the global church in our times. In the words of the *Commitment*'s chief architect, Chris Wright, it expresses 'the conviction of a Movement and the voice of a multitude.'

The Lausanne Movement connects evangelical influencers across regions and across generations: in the church, in ministries and in the workplace. Under God, Lausanne events have often acted as a powerful catalyst; as a result, strategic ideas such as Unreached People Groups, the 10/40 Window, and holistic/integral mission have been introduced to missional thinking. Over 30 specialist Issue Networks now focus on the outworking of the priorities outlined in *The Cape Town Commitment*.

The movement makes available online over 40 years of missional content. Sign up to receive *Lausanne Global Analysis* to your inbox. Watch videos from Lausanne's gatherings. On the website you will also find a complete list of titles in the Lausanne Library.

www.lausanne.org